THE GOSPEL OF **JOHN**

BOOK 1   CHAPTERS 1-10

STUDIES IN THIS SERIES *Available from your Christian bookstore:*

john

BOOK 1   CHAPTERS 1-10

12 DISCUSSIONS FOR GROUP BIBLE STUDY
MARILYN KUNZ &
CATHERINE SCHELL

TYNDALE HOUSE
PUBLISHERS, INC.
WHEATON, ILLINOIS

Bible verses quoted in this guide are taken from the
New American Standard Bible.
Sixth printing, January 1982
Library of Congress Catalog Card Number 78-64487
ISBN 0-8423-1895-X
Originally published as Conversations
with Jesus Christ from the Gospel of John.
Copyright © 1965 by Marilyn Kunz and Catherine Schell.
Revised edition © 1978.
Printed in the United States of America.

contents

Introduction, John

Book 1—John 1-10; (Twelve discussions)

Book 1 of this study guide covers the ministry of Jesus from the time of his baptism by John the Baptist, through periods of increasing conflict with the Jewish religious leaders in Jerusalem. Though the guide is listed as having twelve discussions, many groups will need fourteen sessions for it, since two of the studies probably will take two sessions each.

This study is suitable for groups who already have studied *Mark* and *Acts* in the Neighborhood Bible Studies series, and for groups who are familiar with the Bible and are accustomed to discussion study.

Book 2—John 11-21; (Eleven discussions)

Book 2 covers the events leading up to and including the Passion, death, and resurrection of Jesus Christ. This study is appropriate as a pre-Easter Lenten series of small group discussions for churches, and it is suitable for outreach neighborhood Bible study groups to undertake after completing the Gospel of John, Book 1.

When to Study the Gospel of John

It has been the common practice of many Christians to encourage people beginning a study of the New Testament to start by reading the Gospel of John. However, if you intend to begin a *discussion* Bible study with people who are studying together for the first time, we strongly encourage you to start such a group with the Gospel of Mark, moving next to the Acts of the Apostles. Then your group will be ready to benefit from a study of the Gospel of John.

An adult studying the Bible for the first time will find the text of Mark's Gospel simpler to handle and easier to understand since it is shorter, more direct in style, and uses little symbolism. The Gospel of John is written on two levels. John recounts historical events, but he is also concerned with the deeper meaning of these events, and the significance of all that Jesus said and did. This double level is difficult for newcomers to Bible study to handle, and a beginning group will soon find themselves "in deep waters."

How to Use
This Discussion Guide

Sharing leadership—why and how

Each study guide in the Neighborhood Bible Study series is prepared with the intention that the ordinary adult group will by using this guide be able to rotate the leadership of the discussion. Those who are outgoing in personality are more likely to volunteer to lead first, but within a few weeks it should be possible for almost everyone to have the privilege of directing a discussion session. Everyone, including people who may not yet have committed themselves to Christ, should take a turn in leading by asking the questions from the study guide.

Reasons for this approach are:

(1) The discussion leader will prepare in greater depth than the average participant.

(2) The experience of leading a study stimulates a person to be a better participant in the discussions led by others.

(3) Members of the group which changes discussion leadership weekly tend to feel that the group belongs to everyone in it. It is not "Mr. or Mrs. Smith's Bible study."

(4) The Christian who by reason of spiritual maturity and wider knowledge of the Bible is equipped to be a spiritual leader in the group is set free to *listen* to everyone in the group in a way that is not possible when leading the discussion. He (she) takes his regular turn in leading as it comes around, but if he leads the first study in a series he must guard against the temptation to bring in a great deal of outside knowledge and source material which would make others feel they could not possibly attempt to follow his example of leadership.

For study methods and discussion techniques refer to the first booklet in this series, *How to Start a Neighborhood Bible Study,* as well as to the following suggestions.

How to prepare to participate in a study using this guide

(1) Read through the designated chapter daily during the week. Use it in your daily time of meditation and prayer, asking God to teach you what he has for you in it.

(2) Take two or three of the guide questions each day and try to answer them from the passage. Use these questions as tools to dig deeper into the passage. In this way you can cover all the guide questions before the group discussion.

(3) Use the summary questions to tie together the whole chapter in your thinking.

(4) *As an alternative* to using this study in your daily quiet time, spend at least one hour in sustained study once during the week, using the above suggestions.

How to prepare to lead a study

(1) Follow the above suggestions on preparing to participate in a study. Pray for wisdom and the Holy Spirit's guidance.

(2) Familiarize yourself with the study guide questions until you can rephrase them in your own words if necessary, so you feel comfortable using them in the discussion.

(3) If you are familiar with the questions in the guide, you will be able to skip questions already answered by the group from discussion raised by another question. Try to get the movement of thought in the whole chapter so that you are able to be flexible in using the questions.

(4) Some of the studies will require two sessions. It is *not* recommended that you spend more than two sessions on one discussion. Each session should run from an hour to an hour and a half. Most of the discussions will require only one session, especially if everyone comes well-prepared.

(5) Pray for the ability to guide the discussion with love and understanding. Pray for the members of your group during the week preceding the study you are to lead.

How to lead a study

(1) Begin with a short prayer asking God's help in the study. You may ask another member of the group to pray if you have asked him (her) ahead of time.

(2) Have the Bible portion read aloud by paragraphs (thought units), not verse by verse. It is not necessary for everyone to read aloud or for each to read an equal amount.

(3) Guide the group to discover what the passage says by asking the *discussion questions.* Avoid going woodenly through the study using each and every question. The group will often answer two or three questions in their answers to, and discussion of, one question. Omit those questions already answered. If you cannot discern the meaning of a question, don't use it, or else say to the group that you don't understand the question but they might. If they find it difficult, leave it and try simply to find the main point of the Bible paragraph.

(4) Use the suggestions from the section on *How to encourage everyone to participate.*

(5) Encourage everyone in the group to be honest in self-appraisal. If you are honest in your response to the Scripture, others will tend to be honest also.

(6) Allow time at the end of the discussion to answer the *summary questions* which help to tie the whole study together.

(7) The *afterthoughts* are primarily to stimulate personal reflection on what has been studied together.

(8) Bring the discussion to a close at the end of the time allotted. Close with a prayer relevant to what has been discussed.

How to encourage everyone to participate

(1) Encourage discussion by asking several people to contribute answers to a question. "What do the rest of you think?" or "Is there anything else which could be added?" are ways of encouraging discussion.

(2) Be flexible and skip any questions which do not fit into the discussion as it progresses.

(3) Deal with irrelevant issues by suggesting that the purpose of your study is to discover what is *in the passage*. Suggest an informal chat about tangential or controversial issues after the regular study is dismissed.

(4) Receive all contributions warmly. Never bluntly reject what anyone says, even if you think the answer is incorrect. Instead ask in a friendly manner, "Where did you find that?" or "Is that actually what it says?" or "What do some of the rest of you think?" Allow the group to handle problems together.

(5) Be sure you don't talk too much as the leader. Redirect those questions which are asked you. A discussion should move in the form of an asterisk, back and forth between members, not in the form of a fan, with the discussion always coming back to the leader. The leader is to act as moderator. As members of a group get to know each other better, the discussion will move more freely, progressing from the fan to the asterisk pattern.

(6) Don't be afraid of pauses or long silences. People need time to think about the questions and the passage. Try not to answer your own question—either use an alternate question or move on to another area for discussion.

(7) Watch hesitant members for an indication by facial expression or body posture that they have something to say, and then give them an encouraging nod or speak their names.

(8) Discourage too talkative members from monopolizing the discussion by specifically directing questions to others. If necessary, speak privately to the over-talkative one about the need for discussion rather than lecture in the group, and enlist his aid in encouraging all to participate.

What rules make for an effective discussion?

(1) Everyone in the group should *read the Bible passage* and, if possible, use the study guide in thoughtful *study* of the passage *before* coming to the group meeting.

(2) *Stick to the Bible passage under discussion.* Discover all that you can from this section of John's Gospel. Try to limit

cross-references to those suggested in the study guide so that everyone has the opportunity to study them ahead of time. The person new to the Bible will not be needlessly confused, and you will avoid the danger of taking portions out of context.

(3) *Avoid tangents.* Many different ideas will be brought to mind as you study each chapter of John. If an idea is not dealt with in any detail in a particular chapter, try not to let it occupy long discussion that week. Appoint a recorder in your group to make note of this and other such questions that arise from week to week. As your group studies on in the book of John, you may find some of these questions are dealt with in later chapters.

(4) Since the three-fold purpose of an inductive Bible study is to discover what the Bible portion says, what it means, and how it applies to you, your group should remember that *the Gospel of John is the authority for your study.* The aim of your group should be to discover what John is saying, to discover his message about Jesus.

If you don't like something that John says, be honest enough to admit that you don't like it. Do not rewrite the Bible to make it agree with your ideas. You may say that you do not agree with John, or that you wish he had not said this, but don't try to make him say what he does not say. It is John's account that you are investigating. Let him state his own case about Jesus.

(5) *Apply to your own life what you discover in the study of John's Gospel.* Much of the vitality of any group Bible study depends upon honest sharing on the part of different members of the group. Discoveries made in Bible study should become guides for right action in life situations today.

John states that the intention of his book is "that you may believe that Jesus is the Christ, the Son of God, and that believing you may have life in his name" (20:31). As you study his account, you have the opportunity to face the implications of Jesus' claims for your life.

(6) *Let honesty with love be the attitude of your group toward one another.* Those who do not believe that Jesus is the Christ, the Son of God, should be able to voice their doubts and questions without feeling rejected or feeling that

they should cover up their thinking. Those who do believe and are committed to Jesus as Lord and Savior should be free to share how this belief affects their lives (as appropriate to the section of John under discussion).

Introduction to the Gospel of John

The fourth Gospel, the Gospel according to John, differs in a number of ways from the other three accounts of Jesus' life. The records of Matthew, Mark, and Luke are called the Synoptic Gospels because they give the same general picture of the life of Jesus and contain so much common material that they can be conveniently studied together. A summary is given below in which the Synoptic Gospels and the fourth Gospel are compared.

MATTHEW, MARK, LUKE

They look at Jesus' teaching as it was given to the people of Galilee. They record no visits to Jerusalem or teaching given there except for Jesus' visit as a boy and the last week of his life.

Jesus' teaching is recorded in the form of short sayings and parables relating to scenes and people familiar to villagers and country folk.

Jesus' teaching deals mainly with the kingdom of heaven, its nature, the man-

JOHN

This gospel is mainly concerned with Jesus' teaching in Jerusalem over a three-year period.

It records only a few brief incidents in the life of Jesus outside Jerusalem.

No parables are recorded, though some short sayings are. Jesus' teaching is usually presented in the form of conversations with an individual or a group, or of long discourses either to the disciples or to *the Jews* (the section of the people very doubtful about the truth of

ner of its coming, and the conduct which will fit men to enter it.

Little is said about Jesus' teaching individuals.

Jesus is presented as teaching with authority and making such claims upon his followers as would indicate his position as Messiah, but he says little about his person explicitly.

Jesus' teaching usually is addressed to the ordinary country people of his day.

his claims, or hostile to him).

Jesus' teaching often deals with the relationship between himself and God, and treats themes such as life, light, truth, and love.

Several accounts of some length are given of Jesus' dealings with individuals (but these are still in compressed form, including only the outline of the conversation).

Jesus makes specific claims about who he is and what his relationship is with God.

Jesus' discourses to *the Jews* are addressed to the educated class of the nation. They contain types of argument similar to those used in the schools of the Rabbis of that day.

Material within the Gospel of John indicates that its writer was a Jew of Palestine who was an eyewitness of most of the events presented, and an intimate associate of Jesus. Conservative scholars consider the writer to be the Apostle John, a view supported by the early Christian writers, Polycarp and Irenaeus. His purpose in writing (found in 20:31) is to persuade his readers to have personal belief in Jesus as the Christ, the Son of God. It is generally agreed that the book was written late in the first century, probably about A.D. 90 at Ephesus.

Discussion 1 / John 1

In the Beginning; The Lamb

John begins his Gospel with a Prologue, 1:1-18. While Greek thought may form part of the background of the *Word (Logos),* Jewish thought may be assumed to furnish a major part of its meaning. In the Bible languages the Gospel of John begins with the same equivalent phrase as the book of Genesis, *in the beginning,* and throughout the Gospel constant reference is made to the Old Testament. Considered on its own merits, the Prologue is distinctively Christian, designed to provide an introduction for John's account of the activities and teachings of the One who links eternity and time, Jesus Christ.

John 1:1-18

1. Find and list at least fifteen things said about the Word —who he is and what he does. What does all this add up to?

2. What do you learn about the man named John? What is his task? His testimony?

3. If you had no other portion of the Bible, what would you know about Jesus Christ from these verses? What does a positive response to him involve? What is the result?

4. How does the writer of this Gospel fit Jesus Christ into the message of the Old Testament?

5. Where and why does this interview take place? Describe the questioners, where they come from, who sent them. Look up *Pharisee* in a dictionary.

6. Ask five people in your group to address the five different questions to John, and ask one person to give John's response in each case.

What is John's testimony as to his identity and his job? How does he differentiate between himself and the Christ? Compare with verses 6-8, 15.

7. What does the fact that John is attracting this much attention and is being asked these questions suggest about the extent and the effect of his ministry? (See map on page 61 for location of *Bethany beyond* [east of] the *Jordan.)*

John 1:29-34

8. What is the difference between John the Baptist's ministry and that of the One coming after him? How is John able to identify Jesus as the One greater than he? Compare verses 33 and 6.

9. What do you find particularly striking about John's description of Jesus in this section? See also Isaiah 53:4-8.

John 1:35-42

10. Describe the events of the next day, after John's declaration of Jesus' identity. What do these events reveal about John, his disciples, and Jesus?

11. What deeper significance might you read into Jesus' question in verse 38 and the disciples' response? If you had been one of those disciples, how might you have answered Jesus' question?

12. What change do you observe in Andrew from verse 38 to verse 41 in his understanding of who Jesus is? What do you think motivates Andrew's actions? How persuasive apparently is his testimony to Simon?

13. Note the use of the phrase *the next day* or *the following day* in verses 29, 35, 43. It highlights the rapid movement of events following the inquiry of the Jerusalem delegation about John's identity and his subsequent identification of Jesus as the Lamb of God and the Son of God.

14. Describe Philip and how he tells Nathanael about Jesus. How does Nathanael react?

15. In verse 39 Jesus says, *Come and see.* In verse 46 Philip issues the same invitation to answer Nathanael's objection. Why is this still a valid response to anyone who is hesitantly considering Jesus?

16. What does Jesus recognize about Nathanael? What does Nathanael recognize about Jesus? Why?

17. In answering Nathanael, Jesus refers to the incident in Genesis 28:10-19. What promise does Jesus make to his new disciple?

SUMMARY

1. What most impresses you about John the Baptist?

2. List and define all the titles and all the ways in which Jesus is described or identified in this chapter. Which of these descriptions is most meaningful to you at this point? Why?

AFTERTHOUGHTS

Nathanael, what sort of person were you—without guile, without falseness or deceit? Did you have to try very hard not to be embittered by the false scales and short weights of your day? What did you think when Jesus promised to show you "greater things than these"? Nathanael, how quickly you recognized who Jesus was! I'm thankful for people like you.

Discussion 2 / John 2

At a Party and in the Temple

Following Eastern custom, this wedding would take place in the bridegroom's home, and he, rather than the bride, would be the center of interest. The marriage ceremonies may be prolonged over a period of several days, with the highlight of the festivities being the marriage supper. A marriage and the events connected with it are for the Eastern family one of the most significant times in life. Any lack or failure here would cause acute shame and embarrassment.

John 2:1-11

1. What would be the prevailing atmosphere on such an occasion? What do you know about this home by the fact that Jesus and the disciples are invited to the marriage? On the other hand, what does it indicate about Jesus and the disciples that they are invited to this festive occasion?

2. Ask two members of the group to read aloud the brief conversation between Jesus and his mother.

3. What prompts the conversation? What would this situation mean for the bridegroom? Why does the mother of Jesus turn to him?

4. See John 12:23, 24; 13:1; 17:1, 2 for an understanding of what *hour* Jesus is referring to. What possible connection could there be between his mother's request for wine and his remark that his *hour* has not yet come? Reflect on the meaning of the communion service (John 6:53-57; Matthew 26:26-29; 1 Corinthians 11:25, 26).

5. What is Jesus' mother's response to his answer? How can her remark to the servants be good advice for you?

6. Describe the jars as to number, size, type, and purpose. What connection can you see between the purpose for which the jars are regularly used, the wine, and the hour to which Jesus refers? See Hebrews 1:3.

7. What are Jesus' instructions to the servants? How do they comply? What happens? What does this teach you about obedience to the Lord and the results?

8. How does the author evaluate the incident? How does this incident show the Lord's glory? To what future event in the life of Jesus does this sign (miracle) point?

9. Review the situation. What is the need in the home where the Lord Jesus is a guest? What will likely happen if he does not meet the need? To sin is to fall short. How has the bridegroom fallen short? What is the answer for him? What is the answer in your life?

In a situation which is embarrassing to someone else, how do your actions compare with those of Jesus here?

John 2:12-22

10. Review the history and significance of the Passover in Exodus 12.

11. Compare this incident with the one in 2:1-11 as to place and setting.

12. What does Jesus see, and why does he react as he does? What is Jesus' position in this house?

13. The Temple of God is being profaned by the marketing of livestock for sacrifices and by the money changers' tables where the Roman coins (with their idolatrous images) are exchanged for Jewish coins, for the Temple tax. How would these activities affect the person who has come to worship God?

14. What is the disciples' reaction? What connections are they beginning to make? How is Jesus fulfilling Psalm 69:9? Note the fulfillment also of a messianic prophecy in Malachi 3:1-3.

15. What demand do the Jews make? What does Jesus

claim will be the sign of his authority for his action? To whom does he attribute the destruction? Why do they misunderstand him?

16. When do the disciples come into full understanding of the Scripture (Psalm 69:9, just quoted) and of Jesus' words here?

John 2:23-25

17. What does Jesus' hesitation here to entrust himself to those who "believed" reveal about the quality of their faith? About his knowledge of people?

SUMMARY

1. Compare the two main events in this chapter. In one household Jesus is a guest. In the other he is the "host." How does Jesus respond in each case?

2. Toward what two events in Jesus' life do the two signs or miracles point?

3. Compare the two groups of people who have to do with Jesus in this chapter—those at the wedding party and those in the Temple. What opportunities does each group have and what do they learn?

4. What do the disciples learn from each incident?

5. What Jesus does in these two houses, he does in every life into which he comes. As in the case of the bridegroom he will meet the need, make up the lack. As in the Temple he will cleanse and purify and make fit for the worship of the Lord. Consider if Jesus has done these things in your life. Will you invite him to do so?

AFTERTHOUGHTS

Bridegroom, how did you feel when the steward commented that you had saved the good wine until the end of your wedding feast? Did you rush to ask the servants if they had made a big mistake? What did you think when they told you what really happened? Did you try to keep it quiet because it reflected poorly on you to have run out of wine, or did you gratefully tell others how Jesus had helped you?

Discussion 3 / John 3

An Intellectual

The Pharisees, a zealous sect of Judaism, held tenaciously to the observance of outward rites and ceremonies and the most letter-strict interpretation of the Hebrew law. They superimposed upon the divine law traditional human interpretations, which they held to be of equal authority with the law itself.

John 3:1-11

1. Have verses 1-21 read aloud as a dialogue between Jesus and Nicodemus. Suggest that the rest of the group listen carefully, following the progression of thought and noting the degree of Nicodemus' understanding throughout the conversation. Look for words and phrases which are repeated. From these, what is the central issue with which Jesus is dealing here?

2. What is Nicodemus' position in Israel? What possible reasons may there be for his coming to Jesus at night?

3. What question is implied by Nicodemus' statement in verse 2? What may his use of *we* indicate? What is his attitude toward Jesus? What does Nicodemus acknowledge, and for what reason?

4. How does Jesus answer Nicodemus? What problem does this answer pose for Nicodemus? What does this indicate about his understanding of the kingdom of God?

5. How does Jesus clarify his description of the new birth? In verse 6 what does he say are the results of the two births?

Born of water in verse 5 may refer to baptism symbolizing repentance, or in the light of verse 6 and in the context of Nicodemus' question about reentering a mother's womb, it is possible that Jesus is using water as a symbol of physical birth.

6. What two "kingdoms" is Jesus talking about? What does he say is the way to enter each? See also Ezekiel 36:25-27.

7. What does the illustration of the wind teach about being born of the Spirit? ("Wind" and "Spirit" are the same Greek word, *pneuma.)*

8. What is Nicodemus' response to the explanation? What seems to be his basic problem?

9. What claim does Jesus make for himself, and what accusation does he make against Nicodemus? Considering Nicodemus' own statements in verse 2, why should he accept the words of Jesus?

John 3:12-15

10. Jesus moves from an emphasis on birth to an emphasis on the need for belief. Contrast Nicodemus' desire for understanding with what Jesus says about belief.

11. Ask a member of the group to relate the happenings in Numbers 21:4-9.

Why has this plague come upon the people? What do they ask Moses to do? How does God answer their prayer? Was this answer just as they asked? What does God's method require from each individual? What would have happened to the man who sat in his tent and said, "But how?" See John 3:4, 9.

12. What does the incident from Numbers illustrate? See John 12:32, 33. What does Jesus emphasize as the necessary response? What does he claim is the result of this response?

13. What demand is being made of Nicodemus in this conversation? In what way is this the same demand which the Lord makes of each of us?

John 3:16-21

14. What action has God taken? With what motive and for what purpose? What is the response necessary in order to receive life?

15. What is the contrast drawn between the one who believes in the Son and the one who does not believe? Why do people respond to light and darkness as they do?

16. Notice that the contrast in verses 20, 21 is between the *one who does evil* and the *one who does what is true* (not, "what is good"). What does it mean to do what is true? See 1 John 1:5-10.

John 3:22-36

17. What picture does this section give of the continuing ministry of John the Baptist? What pressures are being put upon him? What is John's answer to those who question him?

18. How does he describe the nature of, and the reason for, his joy? How is verse 30 already taking place for John?

19. What new things are told about Jesus in verses 31-36? How does verse 36 sum up the teaching of this chapter? What two responses to the Son are necessary? What is the result? What is the alternative?

SUMMARY

1. What does it mean to be born anew? What part does faith in Jesus Christ play in this new birth?

2. Why do intellectuals like Nicodemus have difficulty in accepting God's provision? Why is logic not the path to God? If you consider yourself an intellectual, are you willing to sacrifice your "But how?" for belief in what Jesus has said?

3. What is your attitude toward the person who is having intellectual problems as he considers spiritual issues? Observing Jesus' responses to Nicodemus, what should yours be toward such a person?

AFTERTHOUGHTS

John, wasn't it difficult for you to encourage your followers to leave you, to see them start to follow Jesus in-
dependently of you, to see your ministry decreasing? Many
Christian leaders and teachers today seem unwilling to encourage their followers to grow away from them toward Jesus
as Lord. Maybe they don't recognize the issue as clearly as
you did.

Discussion 4 / John 4:1-42

Living Water

Acute antagonism had existed between Jews and Samaritans since the Jews' return from exile in Babylonia. The Samaritans claimed their descent from the ten tribes and maintained that theirs was a pure religion derived from the law of Moses. In Jesus' day, custom held that a man should not speak to a woman publicly; yet in the passage under study, Jesus spoke to a Samaritan woman.

John 4:1-26

1. Locate on the map on page 61: Samaria, the city of Sychar, Judea, Perea, and Galilee. At what point does Jesus leave Judea?

2. To avoid Samaria, Jews traveling from Judea to Galilee often made a detour through the province of Perea. In contrast, what route does Jesus follow on his journey?

3. The sixth hour by Jewish reckoning would be about noon. Describe the setting of the encounter between Jesus and the woman of Samaria.

4. Have the whole conversation read aloud as a dialogue. As the woman addresses Jesus throughout this conversation, trace her progress in understanding who he is.

5. Why is the woman surprised at the request Jesus makes? How would you characterize her response?

6. Beginning with verse 10, what does Jesus talk about? What continues to be the woman's frame of reference? What is Jesus using the well to illustrate? What response is Jesus trying to arouse in the woman? How does she challenge him? List the specific claims Jesus is making.

7. What indicates that Jesus and the woman are talking on two different levels? Why does she want the water Jesus describes?

8. At what point does the woman begin to change her attitude toward Jesus? What element is now brought into the conversation? How does she redirect the conversation at this point? Why?

9. Reflect on how you may prefer to discuss theology rather than your personal sin or need.

10. What would it mean to the woman to have her theological question answered by a prophet? How does Jesus answer her question? What claim does he make? What does it mean to worship God in spirit and in truth? How is it possible for Christians today to fail to do this?

John 4:27-38

11. How do the disciples react to the situation they find on their return? What indicates that the woman is no longer concerned about physical water? To whom does she go and what testimony does she give? How does it affect you to realize that the Lord knows even your secret sin?

12. What is the response to the woman's testimony? What makes her a good witness? Compare in verses 29 and 31 what the woman calls Jesus and what the disciples call him. What opportunity have the disciples had to bear witness to the Lord in Sychar? Contrast what the woman has on her mind and what the disciples had on their minds in Sychar.

13. What teaching does Jesus give the disciples on this occasion? What relation does this teaching have to the incident with the woman?

John 4:39-42

14. What happens to other Samaritans as a result of the woman's testimony? What two reasons are given for their belief in Jesus (verses 39, 41, 42)? How do people today ex-

perience this same sequence in coming to faith in the Lord Jesus? How can you effectively play the woman's part?

SUMMARY

1. How is knowing Jesus Christ the answer to this woman's problems? Why do people today in similar moral and social situations need Jesus Christ rather than reeducation?

2. What is your response to those whose actions are outside the accepted social-ethical standard? Compare your response with that of the Lord Jesus to this woman.

3. Perhaps at least once in your life you have experienced with this woman the harsh realities of social disapproval and ostracism, or with her (she had five husbands) you have known the futile search for security and happiness. Are you also willing to consider and accept the One who promises *living water, a spring of water welling up to eternal life?*

4. Imagine yourself as the Samaritan woman relating your experience years later to a friend. What would you now emphasize? What would you add, and of what would you try to persuade your listener?

AFTERTHOUGHTS

Woman, what happened when you went home? Was the man you had been living with one of those who came to hear Jesus for himself? Or was he threatened by your enthusiasm about Jesus?

Discussion 5 / John 4:43—5:18

A Distressed Parent and a Crippled Man

Though Jesus is generally considered a Galilean, he was born in Judea and was of the tribe of Judah. It is likely, therefore, that the author refers in John 4:44 to the hostility Jesus received in Judea before his departure for Galilee (4:1-4).

John 4:43-54

1. Where does the interview with the official take place? Locate Cana and Capernaum on the map on page 61. How far are Jesus and the official from his home where his son is dying?

2. What has given this father the hope that Jesus can help him?

3. Ask two people to read aloud the brief conversation between Jesus and the father as a dialogue. Suggest that they start with verse 47, reworded as a direct quotation from the distressed father.

4. What is the meaning of Jesus' response in verse 48? What shift is Jesus hoping to see in this man's faith?

5. In verses 49, 50 to what degree is Jesus saying "no" to the father's plea? How can this be applied to some of the answers to prayer you receive?

6. At this point what is required from the father? Imagine yourself in his place. How would you feel?

7. When does the father receive the confirmation of his faith? What further progression in faith follows? What does this family receive in addition to a son restored?

8. How are the claims which Jesus made in Samaria substantiated in this section?

John 5:1-18

9. Where does this incident take place? Picture the scene at the pool. What do you see? What do you hear? What other impressions do you get?

10. Have some of the members of your group read the conversations in verses 6-17 aloud as a play.

11. In verses 6-8, why does Jesus ask the man if he wants to be healed? In his answer, what does the man indicate he believes to be his lack? Compare his situation with that of the sick boy in John 4:43-54. Why would having friends or family not be enough for the crippled man, although he doesn't know it?

12. How does the man comply with Jesus' command to him? (It was against the Jewish law for a man to carry his pallet on the Sabbath.)

13. What opposition does the healed man encounter? In meeting this opposition, what authority does he place above the authority of the Jewish tradition?

14. Where does the healed man meet Jesus again, and about what does Jesus warn him? What may this warning indicate about the reason for his sickness? How do you account for the man's action at this point?

15. How does Jesus' statement in verse 17 answer the Jewish authorities' criticism of his healing on the Sabbath? Why do they determine to kill him? What claims of Jesus are clear from this incident?

16. What are the results, for Jesus and for the crippled man, from their conversations?

SUMMARY

1. Compare the attitudes with which the official and the man at the pool meet Jesus. As you approach Jesus, with which of the two do you more nearly compare? Why?

2. What response is required from the official and from the man at the pool for them to receive what they need from Jesus? How do the two differ in their understanding and faith?

AFTERTHOUGHTS

Man, it is clear why your name isn't mentioned! Why in the world did you get Jesus in trouble when he healed you after you had been sick for thirty-eight years? Did you care so much about what others thought of you that you couldn't be loyal to Jesus? That was really despicable! Who, me? You're asking me if I have done the same thing?

Feb 28/83

Discussion 6 / John 5:19-47

Jesus Defends His Claims

Not only has Jesus healed a crippled man on the Sabbath in Jerusalem, but he claims this healing to be an expression of God's activity, saying, *My Father is working still, and I am working*. The Jewish authorities see Jesus not only as a Sabbath-breaker, but as a man who makes himself equal with God, calling God his Father. Because of this, they seek to kill him.

In the discourse in today's study, Jesus addresses the issue of his relationship to God the Father. Since Jesus' claim to equality with God is a continuing issue in theology today, it is important to give careful attention to this passage.

John 5:19-23

1. Note the emphatic phrase with which Jesus begins his reply to the Jews who oppose him. How does Jesus describe the activities of the Son in relation to those of the Father (verses 19-21)? Who initiates and who follows?

How is this pattern also seen in the relationship of a human father and his son? Suggest examples.

2. What is the Father's attitude toward the Son? What responsibility has the Father handed over completely to the Son? Why?

3. What is Jesus' accusation in verse 23 against those described in verse 18? What does it mean to honor the Son? How is the Father honored? What implications does verse 23b have for today?

John 5:24

4. What phrase indicates that this verse introduces the second major point Jesus makes in his answer to the Jews?

5. What becomes the present possession of one who hears Jesus' message and believes in the Father who sent him? What has happened, and what does not happen, to such a person?

John 5:25-30

6. How does Jesus introduce the third section of his presentation? What time has arrived (verse 25)? What time has yet to come (verses 28, 29)?

Note—Verse 25 seems to refer to spiritual death and verse 28 to physical death.

7. How is the deity of Jesus emphasized in this section? What does it mean to *hear* his voice? What special power is his as *the Son of God?* Along with verse 26, read verse 21.

Note—Jesus is speaking to Jews who have a background of Old Testament knowledge. With verses 21, 26 compare Deuteronomy 32:39 and 2 Kings 5:7.

8. Not only is Jesus the Son of God, but he is also the Son of Man. What special authority and task are his as Son of Man? With verse 27, read verse 22. Why do you think it is as *Son of Man* that Jesus is our judge?

9. What is the outcome for *those who hear* (verse 25) and *those who have done good* (verse 29)? For *those who have done evil* (verse 29)?

10. Though the Father has given him authority as the Son of man to execute judgment, what does Jesus emphasize about his motivation in verse 30, as he did in verse 19? What does this assure about his judgment?

John 5:31-40

11. Note all the references to *testimony* or *witness* in this section. Jesus does not even ask them to accept his own testimony as proof. Instead, what four other witnesses to himself does Jesus point out (verses 32, 33, 36, 37, 39)?

12. How does Jesus describe John the Baptist and his ministry? What does Jesus expect his own deeds to show? What evidence have those in Jerusalem had of Jesus' works?

13. Even though they study the Old Testament Scriptures which speak about him, what attitude do Jesus' listeners have toward him? With what result?

John 5:41-47

14. For what five things does Jesus fault these Jews (verses 42-44)? Give examples of each of these things still practiced today. How would these verses read if each of these faults were corrected?

15. What stern warning does Jesus give his opponents who say they believe the Old Testament Scriptures? What does he indicate about the Old Testament and its purpose? What is the implication of verses 39, 46, 47 for people today?

SUMMARY

1. If you were a reporter covering Jesus' response to the accusations being made against him, what headline would you use in your article? Why?

2. From this section of John's Gospel, how would you answer those who deny the deity of Jesus Christ today?

AFTERTHOUGHTS

Lord, are we willing to stop seeking the praise of other people and value instead the praise that comes from you? What far-reaching implications this choice has!

Discussion 7 / John 6

Physical and Spiritual Food

During his encounter with his opponents in the previous chapter, Jesus made very definite statements about himself. He claimed to say and do only, and whatever, the Father wants. As the Son of God, Jesus is the source of eternal life and as the Son of Man, he has been given the full right to judge mankind. He challenged the people to recognize the testimony to him given by John the Baptist, by his own mighty works, by the Father who sent him, and by the writings of Moses.

(Because of the length of this study, you may wish to spend two sessions on it.)

John 6:1-15

1. After the recent events in Jerusalem, where does Jesus go with his disciples? Why do the crowds follow him?

2. Describe the problem put to Philip, and his response. Suggest a situation today in which you might reply in a similar fashion. How is Andrew's response to the situation different, and yet similar, to Philip's?

3. How would you describe this event the following day to a friend who had not been there? What would you emphasize?

4. What conclusion about Jesus do the people draw from the sign (miracle) he has performed? How does Jesus handle their intended action?

5. Contrast the scene and the atmosphere of the incident in verses 16-21 with that in verses 22-24. How could the testimony of the people in verses 22-24 be used in a court to substantiate the report of the disciples night-time experience on the lake?

6. About what do these people question Jesus? Of what does he accuse them and what command does he give them? How do people today express more concern for the *food which perishes* than for the *food which endures to eternal life?*

7. How does Jesus define the *work* or *labor* which he discusses with them?

8. What do the people say that they need in order to believe in him? By mentioning the manna, what do the Jews indicate about the sort of sign or miracle they want?

9. What does Jesus teach them about the bread from heaven? How do they respond to his description of this bread?

10. What claim does Jesus make? Why would this claim startle them? What have they just said in verse 34? (See also Exodus 3:13, 14.) What two requirements does Jesus make? What accusation does he level against these people?

11. What interrelationship does Jesus describe between himself and the Father and those whom the Father gives him? What is the will of the Father, the work of the Son, and the necessary response from those who will receive life?

12. Review the claims, both direct and indirect, which Jesus makes about his identity and work (verses 25-40). Summarize them in your own words.

march 29/83

13. Why are the Jews offended by these claims of Jesus? What knowledge do they believe they possess? How are people today often blinded by partial knowledge or influenced by "material facts"?

14. How does Jesus answer their murmurings? What does he do rather than deal directly with what they are questioning?

15. What does Jesus say about those who come to him? What promise does he reiterate?

16. What contrast does Jesus draw between himself and the manna in the wilderness? What further clarification does he give about the bread from heaven?

17. What response does Jesus say is necessary for eternal life besides coming, seeing, and believing? How is this response also necessary in order to receive physical life from ordinary bread? Why is bread on the shelf unable to nourish?

(If you wish to study this lesson in two sessions, plan to end the first discussion here.)

John 6:52-59

18. Compare the Jews' response to this teaching with Nicodemus' response in 3:4, 9. What does this reveal about their level of thinking? Compare 6:63.

19. How does Jesus make his assertion in verse 51b even more emphatic? What is true of the person who does not eat the living bread? See also verse 35.

20. How does Jesus explain the spiritual principles of living and abiding? To what relationship does Jesus compare the relationship he has with those who eat his flesh and drink his blood?

21. Consider the many ways in which this bread is superior to the manna.

John 6:60-71

22. The previous paragraphs have described the reactions of the Jewish people to the claims of Jesus. What do some of his

disciples now begin to think and say? Why? Describe comparable reactions today.

23. How would those rate Jesus at this point who say it is important to make the Christian message palatable? What cause for further offense does Jesus mention in verse 62? In verse 63, what does he emphasize is the real meaning of his words in verses 53-58?

24. Note Jesus' insight into people as you compare verse 64 and 2:23-25. What conclusion does Jesus draw about the ability to come to him?

25. How does Jesus challenge the twelve at this point? What effect does his request to rethink their commitment have?

26. In verses 68-71, what poignant contrasts does the writer of this Gospel draw between belief and unbelief? Speaking for the twelve disciples, what clear statement of faith does Simon Peter make? Yet, what disturbing insight does Jesus have about one of their number?

SUMMARY

1. How is Jesus' promise in John 5:20 fulfilled in 6:1-24?

2. Imagine that you are one of the crowd who holds this conversation in verses 25-59 with Jesus. What various emotions do you experience? What conclusion do you personally come to?

3. In what way is eternal life appropriated? What *work* does this involve for you?

4. We live in an age when many are antimaterialists in theory, but materialists in practice. Why is it futile for people to try to satisfy their basic hunger through materialistic means? How has a desire for things or for economic security stood in your way spiritually, or in the way of someone you know?

AFTERTHOUGHTS

Peter, how did you come up with that response? *Lord, to whom shall we go? You have the words of eternal life; and we have believed and have come to know that you are the Holy One of God.* At times the pressures become so great that the strongest believer is tempted to draw back from the cost of being Jesus' disciple. Yet somehow you made the logical spiritual response which helps the rest of us put the issue into proper perspective. There is no one else to whom to go except Jesus.

Discussion 8 / John 7

At the Feast of Tabernacles

The Feast of Tabernacles (literally, the Feast of Booths), the harvest celebration held in late September or early October, commemorates the time of wandering in the wilderness when the children of Israel lived in tents and the Lord provided their food, water, and protection, guiding them on the way by a cloud (pillar) of fire.

John 7:1-13

1. To get a sense of the confusion in Jerusalem about Jesus at this time, ask different individuals to read aloud the actual quotations only in verses 11, 12, 15, 20, 25-27, 31, 35, 36, 40-42.

2. Why is Jesus limiting his Judean ministry at this point? What do Jesus' brothers tell him to do? With what attitude do they seem to make their suggestions?

3. Why is Jesus hated while his brothers are not? When is the church today in the pattern of Jesus' brothers, and when is it in the pattern of Jesus, in relationship to the world?

4. According to verses 10-13, what is the atmosphere in Jerusalem when Jesus arrives there?

John 7:14-24

5. When Jesus begins to teach in the Temple, about the midpoint of the week-long Feast, what is the Jews' reaction to his teaching? What clear claims does Jesus make about the source of his teaching?

6. What tests does Jesus recommend that people use in evaluating him and his teachings (verses 17, 18)?

7. Review the incident described in 5:1-10, 16. The Jews were very strict about keeping the Law of Moses. What inconsistencies on their part does Jesus point out to the people by his questions in verses 19, 23?

8. How does Jesus sum up their problem in verse 24?

John 7:25-36

9. Describe the confusion about Jesus' identity in verses 25-27. Why do some people think that he may be the Christ? Why do they also argue that he cannot be the Christ?

10. How does Jesus address the issue of his identity? How does he indicate that the matter has nothing to do with birthplace or hometown?

11. Compare verses 28, 29 with 5:36-38. What is Jesus saying about himself? What are the reactions to Jesus' claim? Share how you might have reacted if you had been there.

12. How do the religious leaders attempt to solve the problem that Jesus is causing them? What stirs them to action? Consider the spiritual poverty of any group whose leadership responds like this.

13. What do you think is Jesus' purpose in his declaration in verses 33, 34? What speculations do Jesus' hearers make about what he means?

John 7:37-53

Note—As a part of the Feast of Tabernacles, water was brought to the altar of the Temple and poured out each day as an offering in thanksgiving for the gift of water, in memory of God's provision of water on their wilderness journey, and as a prayer for rain in the coming year.

14. The crowd has been whispering and muttering among themselves about Jesus during the Feast. At what point and in what way does Jesus give his climactic invitation (verses 37, 38)?

15. Contrast Jesus' wonderful invitation in verses 37, 38 with his warning in verse 34. What two qualifications are stated in his invitation? Why are awareness of need and confidence in him still necessary for anyone who comes to Jesus?

16. How does the writer of the Gospel interpret the promise of living water?

17. Describe the responses to Jesus' invitation. What divides the people? Give examples of how people are sometimes similarly divided about Jesus today.

18. Have verses 45-53 read aloud as a play. To whom do the religious leaders feel superior? How does Nicodemus challenge his fellow Pharisees? What do they reveal about themselves by the way in which they answer him?

SUMMARY

1. Compare the reactions to Jesus in Jerusalem in chapter 5 with those in this chapter. What do you observe about their intensity?

2. What is the main dispute about Jesus in this chapter? How does this same dispute manifest itself today?

AFTERTHOUGHTS

Nicodemus, were you perspiring when you challenged the Sanhedrin? Did you realize the risk to your position? Challenging the power structure is a dangerous thing to do! Did you argue with yourself, "What I say won't do any good anyway. It could do me harm and won't do Jesus much good"? Do you realize, Nicodemus, the pressures some of us are under today?

Discussion 9 / John 8:1-30

Theologians and the Laity

The *treasury* (8:20) where Jesus spoke was the most public place in the Temple, the colonnade of the Court of the Women, with thirteen treasure chests in which the people put their offerings. Next door was the hall of the Sanhedrin, the Pharisees' headquarters. On the first night of this Feast the four large candelabra in the Court of the Women were lighted to remind the people of God's leading by the pillar of fire. This is the likely background for Jesus' claim in 8:12.

Most reliable early manuscripts omit John 7:53-8:11. Some manuscripts place it elsewhere in John and some in Luke, but there are no grounds for considering it unhistorical and it is accepted as part of the New Testament Scripture.

John 8:1-11

1. Describe the scene in the Temple court. The fact that Jesus is seated indicates that this is a formal teaching session. How is his teaching interrupted? By whom? Why?

2. Why would these religious leaders think that the question they put to Jesus is sure to succeed in giving them a case against him? If Jesus insists on the penalty of the Jewish Law for the adulterer, what will the Roman rulers say since they hold the power of capital punishment? If he refuses to condemn the woman, of what can these "upholders of the Law" accuse Jesus? Note their persistence in verse 7a.

3. How does Jesus' handling of the situation foil their plan to trap him? At the same time, what does he teach these men? What does he teach the woman?

4. Many have speculated about what Jesus wrote on the ground. What do you think he might be writing? How would his writing on the ground help to relieve this woman's humiliation?

5. Describe how you would film the scene in verses 7-11. What various emotions might the departing men exhibit?

6. In later years do you think the woman would consider this day as "the worst day of my life" or "the best day of my life"? Why?

John 8:12-20

7. What is the meaning of the tremendous claim Jesus makes in verse 12? See also 1:4, 5, 9.

8. Compare 8:12 with the claim Jesus made using the same phrase, *I am,* in 6:35. From this, put into your own words what Jesus provides to those who follow him.

9. What argument do the Pharisees use to try to refute the authority of Jesus? In plain terms what are they saying?

10. How does Jesus answer them? Why does he appeal to the Law?

11. What specific claims does Jesus make? What things does he state that they do *not know?*

12. What contrast does Jesus draw between his judgment and the judgment of these strict theologians? See John 7:45-52 and 8:1-11 for examples of their judgment.

13. Why don't the Pharisees arrest Jesus at this point?

John 8:21-30

14. There may be an interval of time between this paragraph and the previous section, and here Jesus seems to be talking with the crowd or the laity rather than with the Pharisees. What contrasts does Jesus mention between himself and those with whom he is talking?

15. What stern warning does he give them? What avenue of escape?

16. What is the meaning of the phrase *I am he* (or, *I Am Who I Am)* in verses 24 and 28? What straight question do the Jews now ask Jesus about his identity? What do you think they reveal by their question?

17. What does Jesus emphasize in his answer to their question?

18. How does Jesus clarify his meaning for them in verses 28-30? Compare verse 28 with 3:14, 15 and 12:32, 33.

19. What is the basis of Jesus' intimate relationship with the Father?

20. How do the people respond in this conversation?

SUMMARY

1. How does Jesus' handling of the situation in 8:2-11 illustrate what he says in verses 15, 16?

2. With what motives do the different people in this study approach Jesus? With what varying motives do people today consider Jesus?

3. As one of the Pharisees, what would you remember about Jesus from your encounter with him in 8:2-9 and his conversation with you in the Treasury in 8:12-20? As one of the crowd in 8:21-30, what strikes you as the major thing Jesus is trying to get across? What is demanded of you in each case?

4. Is Jesus speaking the truth? If he is not a liar, who is he?

AFTERTHOUGHTS

You were the eldest, a position of authority in your society. How did you feel when Jesus challenged your group? *Let him who is without sin among you be the first to throw a stone at her.* Did you realize that what you decided to do would influence the others? Were you embarrassed to acknowledge your sin before them? Sometimes we lack the humility you exhibited.

Discussion 10 / John 8:31-59

Some Tentative Believers

Read the introduction to Discussion 9 for the setting of this section. From verses 30, 31 it seems apparent that the discussion in verses 31-59 is with a group who have expressed acceptance of Jesus' teaching in the Temple. They are evidently tentative believers and interested enough to hear further from Jesus.

John 8:31-38

1. To those expressing tentative belief, what conditions of discipleship does Jesus state? What promise does he make? What are the steps to freedom?

2. What is implied by Jesus' use of the future tense in verse 32? Why do these Jews raise an objection at this point? What are they concerned to protect?

3. Considering their political history, how can the Jews claim that they have never been in bondage? What are the levels of bondage possible for human beings? How is it possible to be in bondage of some sort and yet be unaware of it?

4. What does Jesus teach about the nature of slavery and of freedom? What position and power is he claiming?

5. How does Jesus diagnose their reactions?

John 8:39-47

6. In this section, what two claims of these people does Jesus nullify? How does he reason that their claims cannot be true?

7. Why are these tentative believers becoming so antagonistic? What area of security is Jesus touching?

8. What contrasts are drawn between truth and lies? What drastic statement does Jesus make about their parentage? What does he say about himself?

9. What questions does Jesus ask and then answer?

10. Why can't these people *understand, bear to hear,* or *believe* the truth, his Word (verses 43, 45)? How can this apply today?

11. How are actions said to reveal our true state? What do your actions reveal about your relationship to God?

John 8:48-59

12. If you were painting a mural of this scene, what expressions would you give the faces of the men talking to Jesus? What accusations do they now make? Concerning *Samaritan,* see the introduction to Discussion 4.

13. What is the essence of Jesus' defense?

14. For the meaning of *will never see death* or *will never die* (verse 51), compare Jesus' statements in 8:24 and 5:24.

15. Trace the thinking of Jesus' questioners in verses 52, 53. To what position do they see that his claims lead? How does Jesus answer their questions about his identity and his relationship to Abraham?

16. What claim of Jesus infuriates these Jews to the point of violence? Why? What does this assertion indicate about his birth in Bethlehem?

17. Compare 8:58 with 8:12 and 6:35.

18. Why does this conversation conclude the way it does?

SUMMARY

1. Trace what is said directly and indirectly about *my Father* and *your father*.

2. Why do these people who began well eventually lose out spiritually? What sort of person today has this experience?

3. According to this passage, what are the reasons people do not respond to the truth? How is this the same today?

4. Trace the retrogression of these Jews from being tentative believers in Jesus Christ to being those who seek to kill him. What authority do they prefer before his claims?

5. Think of illustrations of people today who go backward spiritually by holding to tradition instead of continuing in Jesus' word (verse 31). How could this become a danger in your life?

AFTERTHOUGHTS

What happened to you between the time you *believed in him* and the moment that you *took up stones to throw at him?* Were you threatened by Jesus' talk of sin and its enslavement? Was the greatness of his claims more than you could bear? Was it too painful to hear that the truth is found in being Jesus' disciple?

Discussion 11 / John 9

The Blind

The events of this study are set in an atmosphere of deepening conflict between Jesus and the Jewish religious leaders. As background for today's study, review 7:11-14, 25-27, 31, 32, 40-46, noting how Jesus' identity is the topic of continuing conversation among the crowds at the Feast. Read 8:48, 58, 59, noting the most recent confrontation between Jesus and the Jews in the Temple.

John 9:1-12

1. After Jesus slips away from the Temple grounds and those seeking to stone him, what situation does he find? Describe this incident as if you had been one of Jesus' disciples on the scene.
2. The Jews of Jesus' day held that sickness was due to sin. Why then is the problem of one born blind especially interesting to Jesus' disciples? How does Jesus answer their question? Why was this man born blind?
3. How do Jesus' three references to *work* differ? How is the sense of urgency in verse 4 heightened in verse 5?
4. Why would Jesus repeat his claim of 8:12, *I am the light of the world,* in this context?
5. Why do you think Jesus doesn't simply touch this man's eyes to heal them? What would the man's involvement in the actual healing do for his faith?
6. Read aloud verses 8-12 with people taking different parts. Who reacts to this healing? What does the formerly blind man know? What does he not know?

7. As to possible reasons why people bring the healed man to the Pharisees, see 7:31, 32; 9:14, 22.

8. Read aloud this section with one person as narrator and other individuals taking the parts of the healed man, his parents, and the Pharisees.

9. Trace the course of the Pharisees' investigation of this healing (verses 15, 17, 19, 24). Whom do they interview? In what order? What two things do they seek to determine (verses 18, 19)?

10. How do the man's parents handle the Pharisees' questions? What does their reaction indicate about the pressures they face?

Note—The synagogue was a closely knit social and economic unit as well as a religious one.

11. After placing the formerly blind man under a solemn oath to tell the truth *(Give glory to God* or *Give God the praise)*, what testimony do the Pharisees indicate they want to hear? What clear testimony does the man give?

12. Describe how you would feel at the Pharisees' response in verse 26 if you were in this man's place. What are you tempted to do?

13. Note how the healed man switches roles with his interrogators in verses 27-33. Trace the development of his thinking about Jesus from verses 11, 17, 25, 27-33.

14. Outline the steps of the man's argument in verses 30-33. Why do you think his questioners respond to this logic as they do?

15. Review the ways the Pharisees in this chapter refer to Jesus (verses 16, 24, 28, 29). What claims do they make for themselves? Compare with Jesus' warning in 5:45-47.

16. How must the healed man feel at this point (verse 34)?

John 9:35-41   not left to own devices.

17. What initiative does Jesus take when he learns what has happened? Describe the steps of the conversation in verses

Psalm 69:6,7,9
Isaiah 66:5